Unopened

DOUG HOEKSTRA

All selections © 2019 Doug Hoekstra
Five-Minute Books, Inc.

All rights reserved.
ISBN-13: 978-1983664717
ISBN-10: 1983664715

FOREWORD

Ryokan, the 18th century Japanese Zen Monk Poet, once wrote,

Who says my poems are poems?
My poems are not poems at all
Only when you understand that my poems are not poems
Can we begin to talk about poems

Dear Reader:

When I put this collection together, I wanted to frame it as a conversation, something that went beyond throwing a bunch of poems to the wall to create a narrative and allow space for people to jump in. There are poems that rhyme, poems that don't, prose poems, sedokas, and yes, even a sonnet. Some are personal; some are societal. Some look inward, some look outward. Most are pretty recent, but a few go back a ways. As with most art, topics cross-pollinate. Yet, somehow, as I reviewed these poems, I picked up an unconscious thread, hence the three sections of the book. You can read them in sequence, pick one, or mix and match. Choose your own adventure.

Part One is titled "On the Page," because it holds together close to home, with tales of family, friends, and things that center the human soul. Once we are in that place, we move on to Part Two, "Off the Canvas," branching out into the world, natural and manmade, weaving personal, political, and societal experiences. This takes us to Part Three "Between the Notes," where we venture further yet, with tales of music, art, love, and sex, and those indefinable places where we take risks and see where they lead. Once we've done that, we often return to the page. Or not. Your call. But, I do hope you enjoy the journey, and I thank you for reading.

Doug Hoekstra, Nashville Tennessee
https://doughoekstra.wordpress.com/

DEDICATION

As always, this book is dedicated to my son, Jude Aaron Hoekstra. Thank you, Jude, for everything you have taught me from being a father to you.

CREDITS and GRATITUDE

The following selections have appeared elsewhere: "The After Party" (*Deep South*), "Blade Runner Love" (*Feminine Collective*), "Buk" (*Better than Starbucks*), "Dressed in Blue" (*Baseball Bard* and *The Tenth Inning* collection), "Eclipse" (*Second Hand Stories*), "Gravitas" (*Brilliant Flash Fiction*), "In the Direction of the Slide" (*Epiphany*), "Levon and Duck" (*Gambling the Aisle*), "Monday Morning" (*Door is Ajar*), "Ode to the Blue Room" (*Right Hand Pointing*), "Piano Lounge at Wawona" (*Arctic Tusk/Watkins College*), "Stars" (*20 Twenty Journal*), "The Teeterboard" (*Feminine Collective*), "Uphill" (*The Broke Bohemian*), "The Wave" (*Door is Ajar*).

Cover design: Chad Johnson
Cover artwork: Doug Hoekstra
Copy editing assistance: Trey Adams

Thanks also to the following folks for weighing in on the collage/cover art choices: Trey Adams, Stevie Bailey, Shaun Belcher, Lindsey Campbell, Holly Carden, Jude Hoekstra, Ellen Knisley, Pat Meusel, and Corey Mesler.

TABLE OF CONTENTS

On the Page (Centered and Close to Home)

Memory	10
Impermanence	11
Architecture	12
The Teeterboard	13
In the Direction of the Slide	14
Bonie	16
Couples	17
Grotto Falls	18
Inspiration Point	19
Maps	20
Ode to the Blue Room	21
House Concert in Liverpool	22
Killing Time at the Tate	23
Laughter (An Apology)	24
Dressed in Blue	25
Levon and Duck	26
Parental Sedoka	27
Unopened	28
Thanksgiving Day (In My Basement)	29

Off the Canvas (Out into the World)

The First Step	32
Call for Submission	33
All the Way North	34
Grand Observations	35
The Meadows	36
Eclipse	37
The Wave	39
Chance the Gardener	41
The Minimum	42
Officespeak	43
The Claims Approver	44
On My Way to Work	46
Interstate 65 Revisited	47
Progress	48
Rome on Tour	49
Ode to the Sunday Paper	52
Uphill	53
Wheat	55
Stars	57

Between the Notes (Everywhere It Seems)

Bird Watch	60
Don't Touch My Ride	61
The After Party	62
Gravitas	64
Karma	65
Monday Morning	66
Piano Lounge at Wawona	67
Sedoka with Students	68
Buk	69
Collage	70
Blade Runner Love	71
Rio Grande	72
Tarrrget Practice	73
Wistful	74
The Precipice	75
The Radiator Sonnet	76
Vinyl	77
Simplicity	78
Double Rainbow	79
About the Author	81
About the Cover	83

On the Page (Centered and Close to Home)

Memory

is like a dream
and dreams are like memories
chasing you through your days
changing shape
filling holes
until you wake up
a different person than
the day before
which is as it should be
or you would become
thirty thousand versions of yourself
if you're lucky
each crowding the other
keeping the one behind from
moving ahead to
the place you need to be

Impermanence

Visiting my parents
I stay in my childhood home
Which is nothing like my childhood home
In the same way I am nothing like the childhood me
Except when I am

The house is ravaged by time, with chipped wood and worn carpet
Deep scratches in the linoleum where the walkers and wheelchairs
Made their way into our lives
Turning the essence of mid-century dreams
Into twenty-first century disrepair. Different.
Reflecting a journey and a collective state
In the same way they are nothing like my childhood parents
Except when they are

Tonight it's Turner Classic Movies, holding hands and watching
Dancing, singing, and laughing at the Aragon Ballroom
Or the Edgewater Beach Hotel. Chicago.
I see them clearly. Younger. Third-hand memories.
I only know because they told me what it was like
To be stranded in a place with nothing left to plan
In the same way nothing is as it used to be
Except when it is

Architecture

When I am an old man
My world grown smaller like
A childhood home returned
I will close my eyes, smile
Yearn and remember…

My son spread out on the floor
Building with his Legos
His kind and brilliant soul
Wrapped happily into the palm of
His fertile imagination
Doing nothing but knowing

Nothing
Is
Everything

The Teeterboard

Walking by the playground
Where my son used to play
On endless afternoons. Sliding.
Bucket on his head. Pretending
He was the Artful Dodger
Running a hand across the dragon
I noticed

Two children on a seesaw
Or teeter totter; a long
Narrow board with a pivot point or
Sweet spot. In the middle.
A boy and a girl were laughing
As one went up
And the other went down

They bounced and balanced
Perfectly. Power dynamic
Shattered. Equanimity.
Sun dipping behind the clouds
I took another trip around the sun
Sat on a bench and wondered
What happens

On the way to adulthood
And the bedroom
And the board room
And the war room
Where everyone wants their own
And the sweet spot is lost

In the Direction of the Slide

In driver's education,
we watched grainy training films,
sitting in simulators,
which we called stimulators
because we thought it was funny
and we were fifteen

In the stimulators,
a kid on a bicycle would dart
suddenly into the street
we'd hit the fake accelerator
instead of the brake, laugh
and see our score go down

Our distracted gym teacher
was going to pass us anyways,
providing daily advice on IPDA
Identify Predict, Decide, and Act, and
if we hit a slick spot, we should
turn in the direction of the slide

Easier said than done, since
the tendency is to turn the wheel
to the place you want to be
instead of going with the flow
everyone wants something unattainable
especially at fifteen

In the greater Chicagoland area, we had
long gray depressing winters,
sharp cutting winds and mountainous
snow drifts appearing out of nowhere,
clogging city streets before melting into
treacherous slush and ice

So, driving became sliding and
sliding became spinning your wheels,
getting out of the car to push until
someone got out of their car to help
and eventually, together, movement.
Breaking free

It was common to see that same driver
another mile or two down the road,
fighting their own battles, until you pulled over
and helped push, both of you, all of us,
struggling, not learning, not turning,
In the direction of the slide

I used to think my gym teacher was past it,
square, stuck in a job he didn't like,
as he would leave the room, walk outside
and watch birds landing on the football field
but, who knows how to turn the wheel
when you're only fifteen

Bonie

I miss Scotland
and my friends
who took me around
by bus and by foot
through gardens and gargoyles
past castles and river walks
when the rain stopped and
the yellow flowers bloomed
golden across empty glens
deep in the highlands
cutting a path for the ancients
beyond Easter Aquhorthies
and Hotel Portmahomack
where we sang and we danced
and ate our cheese toasties
out on the beach
raising a cloud
in glasses made clear
watching the dolphins
as they swam in the sea
and filled us with gladness
magic and promise
the wisp of tomorrow
I carry today

Couples

Down the corridor there are couples
Different shapes and styles
Seemingly detached, as if walking
On opposite sides of the street,
In the same direction,
Looking down at the pavement
But not at each other
Heading off to meet a teacher
Or sit in the bleachers
The basketball hits the rim. Falls short,
Like the strains of the saxophone
In the marching band's September Song

All children once.

Growing up on different streets
Occasionally alone. Phone
Calling or text messaging
In anxious anticipation
Of a first date that unfolds
With promises of clarity
And love interwoven
Bamboo strands in ancient hands
Carried through the generations
There's a basket by the door
Filled with earnest inspiration
Like the high school play
That needs no second act

Grotto Falls

At Grotto Falls, I offer to take their picture,
A young couple with borrowed camera
She runs a hand through her hair and
He puts one arm around her waist
With calm and clear conviction
I frame the shot carefully in twos

The rocks and river,
The falls and the flowers,
The distance between them,
The distance behind,
The miles one cannot count

I take my time, snapping two for the ages,
Scrapbooks and mantelshelves and
A time when smaller sets of hands
Clutch the frame, asking questions and
The couple smiles with wrinkled eyes
Knowing they have made it

Inspiration Point

Reading dew drops on spider webs like
Fortunetellers in the autumn sun.
Hemlock trees and reflecting streams
Through caves lined with intricate moss
From zoom to panoram we go until
Overlooked by sweeping vistas
Sitting cross cross-legged like Zen masters
on large rocks smoothed by ancient glaciers

This is inspiration point. Deep breath.
We seek in silence. My son asks,
"How many inspiration points have we been to?"
I was thinking the same thing. Three?
But, the reality is greater. Countless
Because every day he inspires me
As I strive to point him in the right direction
Turning every corner without fear

Maps

Carrying maps we move
through battlegrounds and trails,
roadways, displays and
museums built of alabaster
on swamps in cities marked with
European names

Following blue lines, red circles
street signs and highway markers
compass points and scale
measuring distance between places
and distant constellations
that will one day disappear

Slipping into another form
catching glimpses of the future
cherished and held in
our collective past, pressed
between magnetic pages
reframed and then…reclaimed

Pulling on my sleeve, he's
always looking up, always,
even when I lose my way
in all cardinal directions
and happen upon a clearing
beyond my imagination

Where lightning grows quiet and
waterfalls rise and
colors disguise and
the reversal of time
senseless with meaning
perfectly cast together

Ode to the Blue Room

Waiting to enter
The Blue Room to see
Jack White and his band
blast through tracks
from his new album
pounding drums
staccato keys
thrashing guitar
colliding in
a special performance for
a couple hundred Nashvillians
myself included,
I stand in a cell phone free zone
reading the pocket
Thich Nhat Hanh,
the teacher
writing about
the wounded child inside
always trying to get out…
men and women around me
dance, smoke, sway and
I wonder how
this
all
fits
together

House Concert in Liverpool

Punters sitting cross-legged on the floor
the picture taken from
the vantage point of my make-shift stage
two speakers, curtains, blue carpet
rapt attention, strangers and friends
making me feel like home
more home than my home
a blown-out cathedral

Wearing the Paisley shirt I loved but lost
standing in front of frosted windows,
singing songs I knew were
mine alone to quote the McCartney
tune written years after he quit riding
on his fast city bike through Sefton Park
as a young man, not far from the semi-detached
in which I strummed my guitar so sincerely

Killing Time at the Tate

Visiting the Tate Modern
For the umpteenth time
Like all my London shows
Kipping at Luna Simone
Taking the tube from Pimlico
Hours before sound check
Always killing time

Years flash by like reveries
Young love hope beaming
The ones that got away
Old practicing and scheming
Hurry up and wait to
Take another stage
Always waiting for my turn

I come across a sculpture
An old Victrola console,
Painted and displayed with
Shattered 78. Pieces on the floor
Lost friends and broken dreams
Leading me to this place
Always killing time

Laughter (An Apology)

She was like the little sister I never had,
always talking, always asking
always trying…my patience

I was always somewhere else,
never listening, never stopping
never being….in the moment

But I'll always remember driving around in circles
on roundabouts and country roads,
Berwick Upon Tweed and Cobh,
asking directions of the same person
twice
lost and laughing at
our misfortune
in the chill of early autumn

We laughed a lot
We laughed so hard
Together

Dressed in Blue

In the yellow car we rode
All the way to China Basin,
Passing through the shadow of the Mays
"Daddy, see the sailboats,
Underneath the bridge,"
"What's that behind your glasses?
Your eyes," you said, smiling.
"They are brown and beautiful."
Seagulls in the twilight were
Gliding on the wind above the water

The world unfurled before us
Up in the majestic upper deck
Over batters, fielders, true believers,
Sitting on my lap, eating pizza,
Tomato sauce spread across your cheeks
You shouted "Nomar Nomar Nomar, "
Inheriting my Cubness with
Your own sense of style
Smart enough to miss the finish,
Dreaming of a better ninth

As the players left the field
I carried you down the steps
Still sleeping, through the gates
Still waiting, for the Muni
To sweep us back to Union Square
Still wrapped around my neck
Seven blocks to the hotel
Where I tucked you in, still sleeping
My sweet adventure boy
The one and only prince of better times

Levon and Duck

My son takes piano lessons.
I try to teach him
About staying in the pocket but
You know it's a tough year when
Levon Helm and Duck Dunn
Both leave the planet.
I wonder if rock and roll
Will ever swing again.

I wonder who will take their place
And play all night long
For memories, dreams and
Reams of possibilities that
Lie within three chords.
A fourth. A fifth
Suddenly I feel
Like a man out of time.

Backlit darkness
Cherry red cheeks
Long deep breaths and
The climax that peaks
Across silence. Then
Another breath
Before the next dance
Starts up again

I wonder who will take their place
And work all night long
To escape cotton fields
And factories, cast from
Clothes of different colors
To hold on to what we feel
Man, woman, bass, drums
Transcending what is real

Parental Sedoka

Oxygen machine
Wheezing in and out of rhyme
In time with Frank Sinatra
While my mother smiles,
Holding on. My father's hands
Circle hers. Quiet repose.

Unopened

In the unfinished basement
past stainless steel filing cabinets
humming humidifiers and
stacks of yellow magazines
I reach two racks of records
promised to us both

My heart can only take a few, including
"Memories of a Middle-Aged Movie Fan"
by the *other* Ray Charles, unopened,
never played…purchased at Rose Records
for 77 cents, my father killing time
on a 60-minute lunch hour
40 years before.

Thanksgiving Day (In My Basement)

Wrapping my mother's candlewick
In tissue paper, I touch the smooth contours
Of the glass, tracing the curves, closing damp eyes,
Searching for rough edges that have
Suddenly disappeared
The one thing I never thought I'd miss
Envelops me

On Thanksgiving Day, she set the table,
Carefully, with long slender fingers, the hands of
A piano player, singing love songs to my father
Much too marvelous for words,
She reappears
In my lover's dream
As if she was still sitting in her chair
At the end of life
Whispering to me

It's all rough edges, my son
And that's why we celebrate

Off the Canvas (Out into the World)

The First Step

Sometimes the first step is the hardest…

…even when the incline is not so steep, and the switchbacks cross your path, like the mark of Zorro burned onto your ankle at a bad tattoo parlor in a tourist town, you just put on your socks, cover it up, and keep on walking, despite the sweat and the soreness, into a field of promises, until moving becomes easier than standing still and you're filled with curiosity, as the colors of the paintbrush, lilies, and endless open sky tease you like the first time that you meet the lover of your dreams and whatever comes next is everything, it's waiting on the rocky path you're walking, past blankets of wildflowers into a clearing past the pines, where you realize your promise, glimpsing the impossible, a sea of crystal icebergs bobbing in clear water, cradled by the mountains in the middle of summer and you come to close perfection and breathe….

Sometimes the first step is the hardest….

But without it you have nothing

Call for Submission

The anthology stated
"Please, no nature poems."
As if all nature poems
Were of a kind

Duke Ellington once said
There are only two kinds of music
Good music and bad music
I love the Duke, but
Even that is debatable

Since anything of man
Is also of nature,
This must be
A nature poem

All the Way North

Promised rain, we are given
Clouds, dark, expansive and
Welcoming in ways unexpected
Stretching past our field of vision
Over snow-capped mountains in June

Driving on toward Idaho Falls,
I steal glances to my left and think,
"How could this have ever not been enough?"
For those settlers of commerce, solitary riders
Dwarfed by their immense surroundings

Meanwhile an iPod clicks away in the backseat
Like repurposed Morse code, in the hands of
My son. Thunder Road. Piano and voice
Cascade through the burnished twilight.
I steal glances to my right and think

This will always be enough

Grand Observations

Sulfur clouds billow
like warm blankets,
fanned by a distant mother
keeping us alive
do not touch
do not burn yourself,
in these deep hypnotic pools
of emerald and green,
sapphire and blue,
moods ever changing,
on a tightrope wire
ready to blow

The Meadows

As we left the lodge pine forest and
walked through meadows dotted with
yellow wild flowers and patches of blue
we came across a field of ravens
nodding their small black heads to and fro
dancing and hopping in crazy motion
through grasses tall to them, in front of us
everything moving in time to the great sky
opening and closing like a giant bellows
and, for the first time in my life

I could smell the rain

Eclipse

The solar eclipse is coming,
blocking out light for two minutes
turning the world upside down
as it did 99 years ago,
when chickens went to roost
birds went into nests
and the Chicago White Sox
started to think about
conspiring with gamblers
to throw the World Series

In the current climate, I wonder…

Will I drive to a state park, lay down a blanket
under the wide open sky and fill myself with awe,
breathing in and out like a Buddhist monk or
Will you venture to the pyramid-shaped science museum
where a staff of earnest educators and scientists will
wield laser pointers and explain exactly what you're seeing

Will he head up country to the drive-in movie theater,
set up with telescopes and a showing of Close Encounters of
the Third Kind, amongst popcorn girls, and half-moon smiles or
Will she go down town to the baseball game, with its promises of
special edition t-shirts and complimentary viewing glasses
given out by the Mayor and her staff, at the gate in business attire

Will they check in on their neighbors to make sure their cats
don't freak out in sudden darkness, chasing their tails and toys
something everyone should do at least once every 99 years or
Will I cross the street to ring the bell and see if the
newly widowed elderly man needs a ride to the park in
an opportunity to help those less fortunate

Or will we all simply remain anxious about the world
the calls that will come, the work to be done
remaining at our desks, in windowless offices
breathing recirculated air-conditioned air
eyes glued to the computer screen
saving ourselves for the 10 o'clock news

The Wave

The bullpens disappeared
In the offseason
Taken from the fans
And hidden underneath
The bleachers of Wrigley Field
Where deals are sealed
And barons reclaim
The wave - money changing hands,
Adding value to the franchise and
The killing of the filibuster
Brown ivy on the wall, withered
Wiping the canvas clean
Leaving those too young to know
Without a compass

I think of old WGN
Black and white static
Late night Jimmy Stewart,
Mr. Smith and the
Slaying of the Rains,
Following the money
While losing his innocence
Like gourmet popcorn
And flagship stores rising
From the ashes of the
Old Wrigleyville, in sync with
The parting of the classes
Right field sucks, Left field sucks
City boy, country girl
Rich man, poor man.

It was a joyride for the ages
While it lasted. The Cubs
Kicked the curse, while we were
Flattened by the aftermath,
Winning after losing after winning

And what that means to our identity
Me, I'm getting lost in nostalgia
Dollar fifty bleacher seats
Rodney Scott, Pete LaCock
The running of the goat
And the days of negotiation
Because the sunshine's on us all
No matter where you sit…
Or how much you pay to sit there

Chance the Gardener

On the tour, I trace his footsteps.

Movies imitating books, Peter Sellers imitating life
watching flickering screens,
mirroring the moves
losing himself in a kinescope version of
the naked American Dream

When his father died in 1885, George W. Vanderbilt
inherited 12 million dollars,
300 million by twenty-first century standards
spent on opulence he could not maintain
for the sake of entertainment, façade and
numbers, one higher than the other

When her father died, domestic maid number 3
inherited 15-hour workdays,
with a half day off every other Sunday,
spent in the basement of the Biltmore
without a name to be reclaimed,
Shirley MacLaine moans

On the tour I trace their footsteps

The Minimum

Greetings

While standing in line at Walmart buying lights
for my Christmas tree, a matronly voice beckons
over the loudspeaker interrupting my holiday dreams
"Associates to the front, please, associates to the front."

Staff in the break room scatter, blue vests flapping
cigarettes snuffed out in half-empty coke cans
as they race through the door, proudly partnering with
Mr. Walton in a shared quest for success

One for all, all for one. Sam's Club.
Minimum wage millionaires. Spend less.
Minimum wage for you. Get more.
A million for me. Job growth.

The minimum

Officespeak

There is no "I" in team,
But there is no "we" in creativity…
However, if you look closely you'll find
A "me" in team and an "I" in spirituality
There is no "you" in selfless, or
"Everyone" in solitude
Yet, "us" exists in stupendous
And a "bum" lives in umbrella
Proving that it only rains on
Direct reports
Offline, by the
Low-hanging fruit
Resistant to change

The Claims Approver

From behind a
Tiny desk in a
Dusty office on the
Fifteenth floor of a
Massive structure
Set in stone on a
City block
Built before his birth
He paid
Twenty-five thousand claims

Twenty-five thousand claims
In a single year...

Hypertension
Vaginitis
Gangrene
Gout
Rabies
Scabies and
Cancer of the Pancreas
Pulmonary Arteries
Hardening Again
Ptosis
Thrombosis and
Abdominal Pain
He paid
Twenty-five thousand claims

Twenty-five thousand claims
In a single year

From behind his
Coke bottle glasses and
Furrowed brow
He doubled his production and
Hung a picture of his dog and
Waited for his supervisor and
The simple word of thanks
That never came
He paid
Twenty-five thousand claims

On My Way to Work

A middle-aged woman
with faded tattoos,
spills off the bus into the street
holding hands with two small children
who laugh and smile
and look up to her
as if the rain is but a dream

She cradles a grocery bag
as they pass
lingering cars
talking neighbors
distant gunshots
dissolving memory
in the summer air

Interstate 65 Revisited

Eating dinner on the veranda
While waiting for Bob Dylan
The server rearranges
Silverware on an empty table
After bringing me a plate of
Fried green tomatoes
She touches my arm lightly
Answering a question as
Smoke from mountain fires
Drifts into the city like
Gauze over the burning sunset
And factories, some
Abandoned. Fade.
On the highway, where
Signs read "no burn zone"
Drought. Of the mind
Creeps in like the haze
Of lost faith.
Lost practice
Misplaced trust, and
Rusted manhole covers
Rattling through
Burnt Orange America

Progress

At Carl Sandburg's house,
Tourists snap pictures of
Books behind glass
Stacked top to bottom
Downstairs and up
Exactly as the poet left them

Titles beckon as voices from the past,
Tease our collective imagination
Bringing Carl and his family to life.
Inhabitants and possessions
Defined with the times, inseparable
Intriguing, and everlasting

In our world, clutter is disdained
Shunned. A psychological
Condition thrown over for computers
And kindles, presenting a clean slate
Whereas our chaotic realities
Are so much more complicated,
Beautiful
Unique
Fun

Rome on Tour

The gallery. Mirrored glass.
Roman art on tour
Historic heavy metal
Flown in from London town.
Tales of murder, deceit,
Politics. All too familiar
Screaming pick of destiny

Sifting through the rubble
Finding maps and marble,
Silver toothpicks, empty vases
Once held by loving hands
In their homes people gathered
And smiled upon the city
Never imagining its ruins

Cherubs riding dolphins,
Bad art in every era
Flea market thrift stores
Velvet Elvis framed
Dogs playing poker
Obsolescence mastered
Constant reinvention

Through the lens of modern times
Embracing the throwaway
Culture versus vanity
Nero and the emperors
Building bridges, fighting wars,
Naming streets for lovers
In lost pursuit of permanence

Now, they all lay quiet
Stripped of glory and ambition
Another twisted story
Real characters invented
Elevated. Quickly passing
With increasing leisure time
Visiting our end.

Ode to the Sunday Paper

One of my greatest pleasures is
sitting down on Sunday morning
steaming cup of coffee in hand
reading through every section of
the newspaper, curiosity landing
on my lap like the blue jay
at the feeder outside my door
fighting off the squirrels

The New York Times is
delivered to my doorstep
in a blue plastic sleeve to
protect it from rain water and
other unsavory characters,
layered, complex, and changing
it never disappoints or ignores,
bores, or lets me down

This past week, it was
Universal Basic Income
The Mueller Investigation
Renaming the Dinosaurs
Disappearing Coastlines
Consent for Millennials
Parkland Kids vs. the NRA
and the Breeders new album

Sometimes newsprint gets
on my fingers, but words
unfold and let me inside
never turning away, interrupting
or correcting me needlessly
on the length of my fingernails
or the smudge on the rim of my cup
which I accidently missed cleaning

I should throw it away anyways
Because I have too many souvenirs
I'm told, and am too sentimental,
taking too many pictures of things
I love, savoring moments of simple bliss
because they make me feel good and are
worth cherishing like the Sunday paper
which incidentally, never lets me down

Or chastises me for overdressing when
it has worn the same clothes for three days
straight and feels inadequate as a result,
a personal choice and no fault of mine,
the reminder causing a porcelain vase to
fly miraculously across the room
shattering off the wall, accompanied by
barbs bouncing off my chest

Like machine gun arrows on armor,
words typically reserved for dictators
on trial for terrible war crimes
most of the time - I let it go
people are only human
forgiveness is key
kindness is not weakness
everyone makes mistakes

Whether it's a reporter on the beat
or the lover on the run
grace is a white rhinoceros
fighting extinction - however
the Sunday paper doesn't do this
even when it arrives on Saturday night
which is why I'm always glad to see it
and it never lets me down

Uphill

Recently I took a six-mile hike
Up six thousand feet of mountain
Past flowers in bloom, white across the trail
Winding streams and waterfalls
Spilling over cliff faces into beds of
Deep green moss thriving in the shade
During a particular tumultuous political time

East step took me higher, tugging on my knees
And calves, the perpetual pounding heart,
Slow but steady, taking long looks at
Lush forested landscapes kissed by clouds
On the vistas to my left, soaking in the memory
Gripping cable in the rock for footing
The opportunity to catch a little breath
Glad to have no cell service

Soon, I was passed, by a male park ranger,
With a backpack and gun, walking briskly
Unaffected, heading to the top, with the manner of
A gentry on a stroll, up the steps he went
Stones, steps, and stones, increasing every bend
The blood, sweat, and tears of CCC teams
Heroes long since deceased.
Damn, I thought, there are more steps ahead

Next came the gray-haired lady with flowers
On her sweatshirt, passing me both ways
From the overhanging cave to the inspiration point,
Giving little helpful hints as if teaching me
How to bake the best cookies or macramé a quilt
It was the same hiking pack she had in college
She told me with a smile, lips untouched by sweat as
The spring in her steps carried her spryly down the switchback

Several couples followed and whether twenty-five or eighty, it was always
A man with deep etched eyes and baseball cap, on the other side of
Overweight, panting and leaning on his walking stick, still smiling
Clearly gassed, because he would've been passed by his companion
Were it not for good manners and decorum. (I thought about the vote.)
His wife or girlfriend would lightly step in front and behind, as if
In a field of yellow daisies, with a touch of make-up and lipstick
Unmussed by the dust, hair tied back and bobbing on the back of
Her pressed white blouse, perfume carried by the wind into my reddened face
Damn, I thought there are more steps ahead.

And finally, the families, with the matron keeping it together,
One child or two and husband on track, pulling snacks
Out of one bag, water bottles from another,
Patting him on the back, patting her on the back, and always
Pressing on, used to the struggle, the long view, the realization that
Sometimes if you hold back a little, you actually get there first
As long as you can deal with a little pain, see a little sunshine and realize
Childbirth, sacrifice, hurting, recovering, living and dying are what
Makes the world a beautiful place.
I sat on my rock in admiration, got a blast of reception, listened, and thought,
This is why we need more women in the Senate

Wheat

This ain't no oldy-moldy picture of
some holier than thou Madonna looking
down her pretty eye-talian nose at me and
lots of other plainspoken common folk strollin'
through this-here museum on a rainy day in ol'
Kansas City

It ain't no picture of some pre-tentious French
café, frogs drinking weird coffee from tiny cups,
wearin' those funny striped shirts and purple berets
livin' at night and sleepin 'til noon, y'know most of 'em
ain't never been up early enough to see the sun rise slow and
steady over a wide-open plain, if they even have such things in
France

It ain't no mumbo-jumbo hogwash picture full of crazy colors
that don't make sense all thrown together like somethin' I mighta
done myself back in Mrs. Beidelman's first-grade class, the one where
we learned to fingerpaint and I grabbed Mary's blouse she was pretty
even then and got paint all over her chest and had to stand in the
corner,

But anyways, I bet the guy who did this lives in New York City and knows
all the right people, so the rest of the country has to stare at his navel gazin' notions
every time we set foot in a stuffy old museum, which Lord-willin', ain't terribly often
since it don't rain too much in
these parts.

No, this here
is a pretty picture
A picture of wheat
Plain and simple
Golden shocks
Rows and rows of 'em
Each stalk a little bit different
Bendin' in the wind
But still standin' strong
I like that
It reminds me of Mary
Rest her soul
She was so young
I wish the rows could go on forever
But I know it's just a picture
I remember bein' a little boy
On my granddaddy's farm
Runnin' through the wheat
Runnin' after Mary…
This here is
A pretty picture

(for Thomas Hart Benton)

Stars

We
climbed
to
the
highest
peak
in
the
park
so
she
could
put
names
to
stars
that
no
longer
exist

Between The Notes (Everywhere It Seems)

Bird Watch

On the bird watch in the valley
Moving in groups
One person's eyes are another's
Interesting how they tell you to
Never bird walk alone
For just this reason

Interesting was the word
She always used, when
Referring to some untapped
Untried sexual activity,
Testing me again
For some untold reason

Sure enough, I began to see
Things I never saw before
In the light and in the darkness
Because I listened to other
Voices…
Beating wings

Don't Touch My Ride

Don't touch my ride
They used to say
In Memphis town
Back in the day
Pushing buttons
Like a true cliché
No automatic windows to
Box us in.
Roll 'em down
Feel the southern wind
Kiss my lips, feel my pulse
Wondering if
We can see ourselves
In the mirror
When the music plays
Things get close
And we get afraid
Feel the groove
Hear the words
Happiness
Should be deserved
On every block
Of the cityscape
Paint your love
Feel your pain
Summer songs
Ruined days
Don't touch my ride
They used to say
Just walk on by
Like Isaac Hayes

The After Party

At the Orpheum in Memphis,
Waiting for the crew to guide us
Backstage to the after party
I met legendary songwriter
David Porter, and his wife

When soul was soul, there was
McLemore Avenue. Hayes and Porter
Hold On I'm Coming
I Thank You. And later….
I'm Afraid the Masquerade is Over

David was older by that time,
Like all of us, but still hip
With his black leather jacket and
Purple beret, tilted ever so slightly
Still working the angles

When he slipped out to the restroom
His wife just smiled, eyes
Affectionate, knowing, as if
Waiting was something she was
Used to and didn't really mind

"I'm sure you get this all the time"
And there are so many good ones
But what is your favorite
David Porter song?" I asked,
Making conversation notes

Her face became thoughtful
As the stage hands broke down
Rolling and rumbling equipment
Flight cases on casters to the
Unseen side of the stage

"No, I don't get that at all," she said
"But I'd have to choose,
When Something is Wrong With my Baby,"
Past the stage lights she gazed
Searching for the shadow of a young girl

I nodded in agreement,
Thinking of past loves, wrong turns
Destinations lost and found
When something is wrong with my baby
Something is wrong with me

Gravitas

Recently I went out to catch some live music,
Two guys and one girl, laptops and synthesizers
Placed on tables like lab experiments,
Blurting out blasts of processed sound. Patterns.
Interesting for a minute or two. Soon.
I realized it would've been useful to take
Some new club drug I'd never heard of
To fully appreciate
The artistry

Only tools, I thought, and somewhere a genius lurks.
Listening. Watching. Struck by the gravitas
As the performers pushed buttons and stared at screens
Detached. Afraid to connect with the audience
Sway. Living with their parents. Away
From the world. From the love. From the hurt
Come the best kind of trials
Found in the best of
The old songs

I stayed to the end, hoping to miss something,
Went home and put on a Frank Sinatra record and
Danced slowly around the living room with
My lover in my arms. Simple steps.
Smelling her perfume. Shadows on the wall
And, when occasion called,
Looking straight into
Her beautiful blue
Light-hearted
Eyes

Karma

Like a dying man
I lived for the moments
Skin on skin
Touch, kindness
Soft words in dusky light
Creeping through
The shuttered blinds of my bedroom
Like a flip book of memories
Only I could recall
Forwards
Backwards
On we went
Until the space was emptied
Filled with love
And then sadness
As the next day came with
Another piece of change
Emptied from my pockets
And poured into the bank

Monday Morning

Blew through my house like a hurricane of purpose,
Following the wreckage through every room
Cotton balls, moisturizer, tampons lost on the vanity
Deodorant, phone charger found on the kitchen counter
Sketch pad, pencils, poems scattered across the table

Rimbaud, the book I'd bought at a sale weeks before and
Gifted her that day, as we shared another cup of coffee
Her hands wrapped tightly around the now empty souvenir mug
Beckoning me closer from inside, an intimate private joke,
My chalky signature blend laced across its lipstick rim

I take her wool sweater, draped across the chair, and
Carry it to the bedroom, placing it on the futon,
Next to her jeans turned inside out; a found sculpture,
Capped by tank top, underwear, socks, and pajama boxer shorts
Too big for her slender thighs. Too hot. Too much.

Discovering her layers, I smiled,
Knowing there would be more

Piano Lounge at Wawona

She is a grand hotel, white frame veranda
Resplendent with Adirondack chairs
And views of the perfectly manicured lawn,
Verdant meadows, and distant mountains.

The wedding party walks around the fountain
And up the steps, young women dabbed
With makeup, eyeliner and lipstick, glowing
In pursuit of boys ruffled and rustled in their
Black and white tuxedos. Piano chords
Like birds, flutter through the air
And cut through the conversation.

In the lobby he sits underneath sepia shots
Of Teddy Roosevelt and John Muir,
Playing songs that are as solid to the core,
As the granite rising from the valley floor,
Made to last. Gershwin. Cole Porter.

While I sink into the sofa, back lit,
Catching melodies and pondering
What I already knew, that there is
Little in life I love as much as
Music.

Songs well-suited for twilight days
Complete, ye t hopeful and optimistic
"Skylark" is my request; he nods and smiles.
Finds the chord, and plays it beautifully
With Hoagy Carmichael's spirit in the wind

The wedding party crashes up the stairs,
Laughing like bobby soxers and soda
What was I thinking so many years ago?
How did I miss this?
Can I take it all back?

(Thanks Tom Bopp)

Sedoka with Students

Pencils bob upon
Paper torn away in haste
Sails of a forgotten plane
Words from everywhere
Lips without the kisses lost
Hearts alive. The here and now.

Buk

Reading Bukowski
write about cats is
like punching a hole in
a giant bag tied around the world
by those who do not know
but still must classify
categorize and kill
things of beauty

Reading Bukowski
write about writing is
like walking outside our
square box homes, with
First People laughing
knowing, the circle is
the key to the universe
and true peace of mind

Reading Bukowski
write about love is to
see beyond labels like
bum, beat poet, and
dirty old man, feeling
both sides of despair
without false sentiment
or self-consciousness

Collage

Collage is like memory
Random cuts and colors
Pasted and wasted
What you leave out
What you put in
A feeling of lost time
And cherished place

Walking through the odyssey
I saw my Odysseus
On the road for ten years
Making it up on the fly
Through calamity and kindness
With magic arrow
In pursuit of the quest

Only, my hero died
Anonymously slain
On a stage in Memphis,
At a place called the Otherlands
Collage is like memory
I thought he'd live forever
And make his way back home

(For Romare Bearden)

Blade Runner Love

It all started with a kiss
that was something like a dirty bomb
going off unexpectedly
in a populated city
in a movie that I'd seen before
where the survivors walk the streets
but the reaction takes years to dissipate
among the residue,
ticking off seconds on a Geiger counter
while one character tells another,
through eyes filled with pain and longing
that when you love someone,
sometimes that means you have to be a stranger
whether you want to or not.
sometimes that means arriving in a place
unfamiliar; gray colors undefined and
sharp points around every corner,
cutting deep, often wounding, always
past, present, and future, I watched
a strange sixth sense develop, as
blanks fired into a dystopian landscape
two people fighting to the end of love
not even sure if the end could ever be
and like my favorite poet's song,
kiss still lingering, I knew
someone had to tell the tale and
I guess that it was up to me

Rio Grande

In the darkness of my bedroom,
watching Rio Grande with its
flickering shadows
dissipating dust
and
Ben Johnson
roman riding
against the open sky and
sandstone spires of
Monument Valley…

I think of her.

the vacation that she planned
and never took
only to find out

it wasn't Monument Valley at all

Tarrrget Practice

"I was just doing a little tarrrget practice," the hero shouted to the angry mob, in a pretentious Irish brogue, as he ran down the rickety stairs of the sea-worn dock and tossed his gun into the mysterious murky water.

'What's going to happen now?', she asked, the words falling from her lips to her body, as I squeezed her tight and her blood beat hard and the rhythm swelled as we stared into black and white shards of broken light.

I wasn't about to let her know I'd seen this one before, stumbling through the dark alone, tripping through grey shadows and rain-filled nights chased by misadventure and poor judgment, not unlike this careless hero.

"I was just doing a little target practice," I whispered soft and low as the cymbals crashed and the credits rolled and I thought about the days that came and went before and how they, too, had to be tossed away for the climax to arrive.

(*For Orson Welles*)

Wistful

Lightly on my arm,
Softly on her lips
I watch her fingers trail,
Leaving small drops of
Possibility,
Falling silently
Into a place
Between us
Unmistakable
Present
Real
The smallest of gestures
The lightest of words
Awash with a feeling
After goodbyes
I carry my broken smile
To darkness and dreams
The crossing I will never make
Because it is this time
And not another.

The Precipice

Middle
age
came
when
it
suddenly
became
difficult
to
choose
between
hot
murky
sex
and
a
cool
clear
mind

The Radiator Sonnet

The radiator wretches, kicks and clanks,
working its whisper into a roar,
blowing its steam into a bank
of cascading bars. The bedroom floor
is covered with clothes shorn and thrown
from passion to lust, where a long slow
kiss cries with ever rising moans
and strikes a match for the after smoke.
She dove like a dove into her dreams,
undaunted by this crank old
radiator bent on awakening me,
keeping us both from the cold.
No sense in shaking her soft soft slumber,
I pull back the covers and play with my lumber.

Vinyl

Lately I've been
Listening to old records,
Guilty pleasures
Lovingly encased in plastic,
Stored away in dusty places
I never thought I'd visit again…

Unwittingly the needle drops,
Bringing back moments
Painted and cast
Anticipated nights
Long drives long forgotten
Girls and worlds, to be touched again

It's funny how a chord or
A melody that lingers
Brings you back in time
Effortlessly. Moon River.
Wichita Lineman. Songs
I didn't even know I liked

Can make me cry
Even when they skip
Nostalgia fades away
But I still can't understand
The boy who was standing
In the mirror so many years ago

Simplicity (Poem Written in High School)

I love the sound of breaking glass,
especially when I'm lonely
people who understand,
those who are distinctive

A radio playing softly at night, barely audible
A gentle breeze blowing through an open porch
A single smile in a sea of strangers,
The beginning of the late show
The middle of the dawn
Any thought that comes my way
Much too simple to explain

Double Rainbow

Driving on towards solitude
listening to Edward Abbey read
against a backdrop of desert hues
worthy of a painter's palette,
my son and I share the
words, visions, experience
from opposite ends of the spectrum
He, starting at the beginning
Me, heading towards the end

with a sense of perspective,
and proportion
two ravens land on a Pinyon Tree
standing alone in the distance,
defying the odds,
framed by looming sandstone cliffs
and a double rainbow that appears
seemingly
just for us

ABOUT THE AUTHOR

Doug Hoekstra is a Chicago-bred, Nashville-based writer who lives the Music City with his son, Jude.

Educated at DePaul University (B.A.) and Belmont University (M.Ed.), Hoekstra's first book, *Bothering the Coffee Drinkers*, appeared on the Canopic Publishing (TN) imprint in April 2006 and earned an Independent Publisher Award (IPPY) for Best Short Fiction (Bronze Medal). As *Paste Magazine* noted, "Music runs like a liquid vein through these 80-proof experiences. Hoekstra pours it out with a Dylan-esque fervor, giving us a sputtering catalog of beauties and terrors…" A second book of Hoekstra prose, *The Tenth Inning*, was released independently in 2015.

As a musician and songwriter, Hoekstra has also written, arranged, recorded, and released nine CDs of original material on labels on both sides of the pond, touring most of the continental U.S., as well as several Europe countries, performing at bookstores, coffeehouses, clubs, libraries, pubs, festivals, and castles, solo and with band in tow. Past highlights included Nashville Music Award and Independent Music Award nominations, lots of Top 10 lists, cool live radio (a regular on Acoustic Cafe, World Cafe, BBC England, BBC Scotland, and more) and many groovy times. "A lot of people write songs, Hoekstra writes five-minute worlds" (*Wired Magazine*).

https://doughoekstra.wordpress.com/

ABOUT THE COVER

As I re-read these poems, I was reminded of the obvious—perception is reality, colored by one's experiences, taking on new life when one tells a story or brings another person and their experiences into the conversation. Art bears witness to this, but often reveals itself as a collection of fragments—memory, imagination, anticipation—broken, reassembled, and made whole. So, I thought the cover of this book should reflect that.

There are two poems in the collection that are central to its whole—the title poem, "Unopened," which centers on my father and pivots off an old LP I recovered, and "Thanksgiving Day," which centers on my mother and pivots off some of her old glassware—candlewick. My concept was to take images representative of those poems, break them and put them back together, so they became, like the narratives, both real and imagined, both literal and abstract.

First, I took photographs of the album cover, printed those in various sizes, slicing and splicing the pieces randomly on different colored backdrops, like found sound, working through about a dozen iterations. Then I photographed two candlewick glasses and printed those images on transparency paper, in different sizes, smearing the ink as it came out of the printer, again about a dozen versions. Then I mixed and matched, laying the various transparencies over the various collages, scanning and manipulating those layered combinations again.

So, in the end, the source images were represented in full, but modified by experience, and as in life, memory, imagination, or poetry, certain images or themes rose to the forefront. From that point, my friend Chad Johnson assisted with the graphic design and made the images work with the context of a book cover. While I'm not a visual artist per se, I am enamoured by the results, and I hope you enjoy the personal if rough-hewn touch it provides, seeing it as a worthy mirror to the words inside and the journey we share.

Thanks for the read and the view…

Doug Hoekstra

Made in the USA
Columbia, SC
17 October 2018